Local Interest

Local Interest

Emily Hasler

First published 2023 by
Liverpool University Press
4 Cambridge Street
Liverpool
L69 7ZU

British Library Cataloguing-in-Publication data
A British Library CIP record is available

ISBN 978-1-80207-814-5 softback

Typeset by lexisbooks.com, Derby
Printed and bound in Poland by Booksfactory.co.uk

Contents

A Mud

is a singular creature
of variable size
with a great many mouths.

It can smack and suck its lips
but mostly stays schtum,
sticks around quietly.

It adores a Water,
and they mingle parts
twice daily,

then roll away and lie
prone and touching,
the scent of each rising

into an Air (a whole other story).

The Flooded Field

A breach exists:
field is flooded,
is not field.
Mud is admixture
of sleeping and waking:
forgets objects, uncovers them.

A breach in the seawall does not
exist, is not a thing
but an unmaking:
unmaking more and more
with each tide
gulping
uncoming less:
spitting it out.
And it's here the cormorants
revel with and against.
A tyre is more or less visible.

\ /
/ \

Field is not flooded.
Flood cannot be always:
is surprise/mistake/aberration
not twice daily.
Unfield is: marbled silt and mud,
salt trees, strung wire,
stricken telegraph posts.
Was-sheep, was-cows,
wader throng, egret stalk.
Is lug and slump just to look at.
Is impossible-full of legless, uneyed life.

Is impossible: they have undertaken
to repair the breach.

\ /
/ \

Unfield is only just beginning:
wrinkled as a babe,
twizzled veiny,
burbling. Faint pock-pock,
of air escaping at full ebb,
the lowest rolling boil.
Beside the deepest channel
where water enters first
and hardest
the banks are building:
dirty baize of algae
catching the sediment.
And also around
the abandoned water trough:
algae, grass.

\ /
/ \

Scour and drag
inhales workmanlike:
see, what you need...
for the water to keep
coming
but to bring more than it takes;
for a calm day
lasting half a decade.
The fences lean, consider.

Water tongues at all possible pain,
it's not an unpleasant sensation:
pressure on the wound
which isn't there yet,
salt on the cut.

\ /
/ \

People forget.
Before the flood...
a barn owl hunting?

Field remembers:
tyre marks remain
from the reccy the engineers did,
carefully crawling a vehicle,
entering by the old gate.
The old ditch lines are still visible,
the fences still more or less stand.
But the breach was always there,
air waiting to be reclaimed.

\ /
/ \

When this land was first inned
is beyond the maps
which all show the same shape
and the feathering marks
for dyke or defence:
a row of pikes primed.

Before the seawall
there were a great many breaches
living peacefully in coexistence
with the tides: not land, not water,
a great muddiness, a prospect, a waste.

4

\ /
/ \

In this corner
thorn bushes have died
a salt death,
leafless but lived in:
sparrows chatting,
whispers of sediment
round the roots.

\ /
/ \

Field is creased,
the extra folds
where the bent wrist supports
the hmming head
and a line appears
which needn't have been there
but now it is—a rut,
and there the thoughts run:
habit(at)-forming.
So it is: chance become
geography. So it is so it is.

\ /
/ \

You want to touch the mud:
its cool smoothness
its grainy warmth
and thick stench.
The ducks dabble here:
you can see it on them
and in the silty shite
that passes through them.

Below the mellow surface
a darker brew:
anoxic, sticky with
cyanobacterial glue.

\ /
/ \

The wall is long,
tallish, fairly wide,
but breach is bigger.
Breach's volume is all
it lets through:
here realities flocculate.
Some come to nothing.

\ /
/ \

The breach persists.
It is/has been/
can be again.
A fence has been erected:
Keep Out.
Climb over:
walk along to the breach,
or where the breach was,
through every breach
that was and could be.

Inventory for a Poem
with Panoramic History

10 consecutive hot summers
9 bagged dogshits
8 CDs on string
7 sets of Woolworths crockery
6 pieces of oasis
The fifth rebuilding of the bridge
4 prosecutions for smuggling in 1751
His third wife, like the first, died from exposure to the bad
    marsh air
Two horse land
A one-night house

At Cobbold Point

At Cobbold Point the water moves in more than one direction.
I swim between imported Norwegian rocks which pin the shore
in place and think *for the most part the coast is accreting rather
than eroding*. The breakwater like a curved spine/my curved spine
breaking the water. I am accreting thoughts, the coast for the most
part and, rather than eroding, I hang in the water at full crawl
trying to guess where the last Dutch invasion force landed. This
is complicated by the sea defences and the erosion of the original Point.
The coast, for the most part, is thinking, accreting rather than eroding;
so that nothing is really lost, just reconfigured. Two thousand Dutch
    marines
marching up the prom, past the ornamental gardens, chanting: *accreting
rather than thinking*. Coasting the erosion, for the most part, I think
I understand my limits, but where the sea meets the breakwater there's
no knowing the undertow. On a clear day you can see Sealand. You
cannot see the Roman castle, submerged one mile out, but I feel it
between my toes. Accretions of erosions I think, most parts. Coast is
what I swim, is what I think, moving in more than one direction.
My coast, imported Norwegian rocks for the most part, will hold,
I think, accreting rather than eroding, here at Cobbold Point.

Forster's Tern

The birders—yes—
flock to see it.
What's a Forster's tern
but a leggier Common tern?
And what's a tern but a gull
in italics?
It's the dynamics
of the group that captivate;
the unknowable journeys
of enthusiasm.

Drove

On that bare brown field
seven clods came to life and
—like that heavy clay
would marl itself—
began to flee and fight,
breaking endlessly without
breaking apart
the group—the drove.
In frenzy. We watched
from the other side
of a hedge. The world
was shuddering on the leeside
of its crux, the loose ribbon
of peninsula ruffled still...
but no, not moon-
struck—self-disturbed
hares leap from the earth.

Gloss

For Michelle

This was before the playing fields were sold off.
We took that scuffed pitch for granted,
week in, week out. There was the trainer smell and squeak
of the sports hall and, come the allotted season,
six weeks' rugby. Touch only, but in secret
we had agreed to play *properly*.
It wasn't raining, but it had been, and no sooner
had we stepped on the turf than it slipped
beneath us. I don't remember the teams,
or the teacher, or a ball—just a bunch of girls
testing every side of themselves
against every side of the ground
until the foxy mud was slick enough
to coat our dry-shaved legs, until we were
rolling around in a mire of our own making.
Was that portion of earth ours? We flung
it anyway, that afternoon, though we knew,
full well, the showers didn't work.
Because we knew how to play properly.
Walking home, our smiles cracked
but in that moment we shone like teeth.

Deaths

When the cormorant came to die I told it
what I felt. For a week it scooted the pool,
dipping its neck for fish, unable to dive.
Unable to fly, it remained.

                Unable to perch
it sat awkwardly on the duckshit-enriched
wooden platform. Unable to live, it died.
We lifted that used body with a spade,
laid it on the salt marsh side.

              Before this
there was the case of the disappearing
ducklings. Later, the oxygen was ripped
from the river and with it so many fish.
Later still,

           a lone teal crouched in the reeds
until it didn't. Meanwhile, duckweed proliferates.
The night we were told E had died I thought
I heard an otter's strange warm squeaks.
I couldn't be sure.

             We never diagnosed
the cormorant. Petrol-black, warning-yellow beak,
a green eye—always I see it in profile. I said
I love you, meaning *Distance is impossible*,
meaning *I will not wish for it.*

The Age of Coastal Sail

Is over.
You must understand before we begin.
We barely knew it existed until it was ending.
Of course there were photos and oral histories.
But every one was the last in some way.
And lasts are different.
Like horizons in haar.
Or the memory of a house lost to the sea.
Swollen out of shape with meaning.
Salt. Plenty. Beamy.
Run a finger down the coastline.
Remember its riddled hull.
The creeks and ports shift beneath the pressure.
We want to learn knots and all the names for boats.
It is not what it once was.
Here was the water.
This must have been land.
It seems we're stranded.
Our beaches accumulate in eternal off-season.
Only on the slack do you catch someone telling someone else:
Oh yes you just missed her.
There she goes.
No? Can you see?

Here Be Dragons

Between the cursus and
the Stour, a kettle hole.
Wormingford Mere, formed
like a pearl around a stubborn
block of Ipswichian ice.

1981: The Cambridge
Department of Botany takes
a two inch core of sediment
from the centre, where the
water is 20 feet deep.

They find 30 feet of soft
dark mud, and, under that,
17 feet of mud—dry, hard,
compact. Below this they
cannot go. The bore is lost
before it can reach

the bottom and whatever
lurks beneath the tell-tale
pollen they find at 47 feet:
a landscape of hazel and
birch, some elm.

9,000 years later, give or take, the lake is private, a Heras fence blocking the entrance to the spirit world. But the map shows the shape— *lymnocryptes minimus.* A Jack snipe, little dragon crouched between earth and flight.

Don the Diver

William Portuge
puts on the diving suit
and the name.
Both are simple
but unwieldy.

The improvised
air apparatus is designed by
our very own
Mssrs Lewis of Harwich,
states the handbill.
Understand: it's a stunt.

Noon: he is about
to embark or rather
disembark, for he lowers
himself from a vessel to walk
to Shotley Gate across
the estuary's riverbed.

It is not recorded
if he greets the crowd,
which, despite his fame,
is not so large
as many thought
the whole thing a hoax.

Still, there are
boatloads of spectators
to cross with him
to the Suffolk side.
But what is there to spectate?

A double reef breeze

furrows the water,
so it is neither a window
or a mirror but
a black velvet cloak.

And anyway
the water here
has always colluded
with the earth
so Don himself—
if Don he is down there—
can barely see
and with each step
makes the way ahead
less clear.

Oh well, sometimes
it is better not to look.
Imagine unevenness,
obstacles, the clanking
heaviness of the suit,
the chugging propulsion

of that oh-so-Victorian
faith in progress.
Imagine gasping.
It will take one hour,
twenty minutes.
There will be cheers
for the 'undaunted Don'

and suggestions
that come the regatta
he'll walk the whole

of Orwell Haven.
And no one will see
that either, and there'll be
no record if it was done,
and I don't know
what became of William.

Doggerlander

For Elley

They're there, in Doggerland.
We cannot see them
for the murk of the North Sea
and millennia, the people who
hunted and gathered there,
who moved with herds of deer,
who found their camp submerged
and decided to rebuild. We cannot
know the girl who sits beside
what we will call the Shotton River
but to her is just whatever 'river' means.
We cannot know if she picks and chews
a blade of grass, and if she finds it
sweet or bitter. Oh yes, life is hard,
hard and short and full of fear.
The sun warms her left arm,
a breeze lifts the hairs on her right.
She feels the wings of something
pass close by her face
and with a fingernail works a thorn
from where it has embedded itself
under the skin of her palm.
The river pelts past like running deer.
A twig snaps and her ear traverses
the woods on the opposite bank.
Far enough for now. She finds
her hands have twined together
two strands of grass and lays
the braided circle on the ground

before she walks away. A shift
in the wind, coarser now. She sticks
her tongue out: salt, perhaps.

Survivors of the East Coast Floods

who wake in the dark
to *once every thousand years*
rising through the floorboards /
who live in all unlikelihood / who
overhear the plot between pressure,
tide-range, wind-drift, sea-fetch /
who understand the water / but cannot
trust the earth beneath them /
who fear the arrival of Arctic winds /
the unreliability of the nearest star /
and our own dear traitorous moon /
who know time does not flow
or ebb only / but will find a way /
up creeks and estuaries /
to rush in / overtop the river banks
while you look to the sea /
keeping watch for the future

Limit of Range

Fingringhoe Wick, 19 March 2019

They are skulking and extremely local in their distribution
                                                    RSPB website

I arrive before the nightingales (assuming they will arrive).
And before me came the Romans (who came by water (always
in the way (in this fiddly estuary (they found ideal for trade))))
and before them was the Ice Age (that laid down the gravel
(which was dug from the pits (and made this landscape
(with its scrub and trees not meeting (the type of woodness
that will not support bluebells) perfect for nightingales)))).
Behind me is the firing range (arrhythmic (intermittent)
        chattering),
and all around the blackthorn in bloom (in case you're
        interested
(I've already assumed you're interested) in such vital specifics
(the gorse in flower (always), the first brimstone of the year
(waving itself like a flag))). I am local (ish (it took me a while
to get here (since I cannot fly (and there's all that water
(which the Romans found useful (and was used to wash
the sand and ballast (from the last Ice Age) which was dug
from the pits)))))) but I took the long way (the only way)
        round.
And they are local (and foreign (and familiar (and rare))),
this place is famous for them (but they are not here (yet)).

Superstant

You take a bit of crepe
to pin to the skep,
and you go down,
and tap on very gently,
and you tell them who has died.
And though no one has died,
so much has changed
that you want to tell the bees.
You want to say sorry
for the shifting and the strange
new way you speak,
carefully unloving. Dear bees,
you are no less dear. But I must
go round, recalling rituals,
tap on, tell everything—even
the bees we never kept,
which thrum along almost
no differently, leaving
no paths in the air.

Wrabness

For Jane and David

We met there on holiday,
oh a lifetime ago...

Which is not so long.

It can be measured
in the slow-slow-quick

crumble of red cliffs

that sometimes will loose
animals that moved

in ages we give

strangely local names
and formed the sands and clays

on which you holidayed.

You could count it in summers,
in visits to that beach hut,

not a forever structure—

but lasting enough.
Life is a beach—

the point at which

the sand in the egg timer
seems to hold still.

Suffolk Girls

Stolen from Richard Cobbold's The History of Margaret Catchpole

fiery little animal
strong bone, short joints, clean legs
stout chests, high crests
fiery little
will kick and plunge
will give full play to lungs and legs
strong and well-knit limbs
accustomed to the heaviest of labour
this wild little home-bred nag
her bonnet hanging down behind her
something between a cart-horse and a roadster
this brute was like a donkey in one respect
a high-spirited little horse, and aged
the old pony of her master's
two noble horses that are worth riding
a fiery grey horse
a strawberry roan
free easy gentle noble swift
untiring graceful and grand
the horse is stolen
a cut tail and is very strong and very fast
the finest shaped horse I had ever seen
It is the very horse!
the remarkable character of the horse
willing steed
the animal exhibited
Did you ever see a better shape?
there's a crest—there's a shoulder—there's a head!

legs, as straight and clean as a colt's
not every man's horse
Not easily matched
the very horse!
a charming shaped horse...
tall and rather slender
a dark eye, dark hair
the large linen-horses belonging to the gaol
the chevaux-de-frize
clever, shrewd, and well-behaved
would make a very bad companion for any man

Smugglers

Let's play smugglers, you say.
I say, It's been romanticised beyond all recognition.
You're no fun, you say.
I say, The bare facts are quite sufficiently dramatic and colourful.
The clandestine sinking of contraband in creeks and estuaries, you say.
I say, That comes later; at first cargoes were run on to the beach.
Undercover of dark, you say.
I say, In broad daylight.
Oh, you say.
I don't think you understand the game.

Starfish

We could find no trace
of the decoy site
which was made to look
like the port had been
bombed, like the port was
on fire, though there
was no port and the
fire was controlled,
bracketed, contained.

*

We do not find it:
Starfish—to be seen
as fire from sky,
like fire thinking
of itself seen from
the sky. It's cold so
trill your fingers beat
beat beat beat beat your
numbing/thawing toes.

*

Because from the air
one estuary is
much like another—
same differences.
Arms of land creeping
into the sea at
night limbs wandering.

*

The map was unclear.
Not by the—*in the*
spinney. Actually
we're already there,
decoy (where it was)
now low-lying marsh.
Cuts frozen partly,
crazed ice creaking burns
to the touch I think.

*

But I digress. The
decoy site was all
around us, we just
did not make its cen
-tre, bunker, oper-
ations, its central
escape hatch ingress
egress now replaced
with a skylight. In
the arms of the beast
sought warmth, drumming five
fingers for feeling.

*

The last I saw was
gull-gotten, pulled a-
part with no regard
for that unique sym-
metry. Same diff'rence.

*

A penalty laid
on those engaged in
oyster fishery

who do not tread on
or throw upon the
shore, a fish which they
call Five-finger, re-
sembling a spur-
rowel, because that
fish gets into the
oysters when they gape
and sucks them out. Out.
Chemical control,
caustic action, quick-
lime, lesions which pen-
etrate and spread like...

*

Decoy pond—quisling
ducks, the trap shuts shut.
Controlled fire. You stum-
ble upon them, you
can't resist: Decoy
Pond, Mill Hill, East Lane,
Decoy Pond, Mill Lane,
East Hill, Decoy Hill,
Mill Pond, East Lane. All
quiet all quiet
yes as you were now.

*

As per diagram:
See here. And this. Burn.
Land: to land a fish.
Reel: to reel back,
to reel in, a
dance, a diversion.

*

My lower case Rs
split at the seam lit-
tle diff'rence between
fire and five. Fi—re!

*

Torn apart but not
any old how. Loosed
between spicules,
between ampulla,
bulging waterways
in the animal.
Everything has its
perforations its
raggedy edge which
is weak which begs to
be exposed—what it
burns down to at last.

*

These flexible spines,
these waterways. See
how this estuary
looks like the other?
Same differences.
You know, don't you, what
a flame looks like? Draw
me a star. Five flames
Star finger. Gull. Look
harder. Look until
you see double till
you see quintuple.

*

We could find no trace
of the of the of the
we could find no trace...
Same difference same
feeling about in
the light. Thrown by rays.

*

Starfish are all branch-
ing. Arms covered in
legs. *Spines—Noun, plural:*
More or less movab
-le outgrowths of cal-
careous plates forming
the skeleton and
enabling the
starfish to ward off
its predators. Fire.

*

The coast is spined with
fortifications,
they crumble along
predictably un-
predictable lines.
'Factories', 'houses'
you must imagine
the whole town if you
want to make it burn.
Hullo yes I am
already on fire.
All five fingers all
present and correct,

we're all here burning
in the cold daylight,
do you see us now
hiding in our shells?

Erosion and Deposition

Landscape
Landscap
Landskep
Landskip
Landschipe
Landship
Ship
Ship
Ship
Shipland
Schipeland
Skipland
Skepland
Scapland
Scapeland

The Labours of the Months

October

The noisy pylon
is embattled with starlings,
sharp as anti-bird spikes.
All at once, they decide
to communicate themselves
away.

November

Wildfowl arrive
to remind us
it could be colder
and darker still.
By two the day has already had it
and even more terrible things happen,
so we start to make plans
for New Year.
I must be ducked regularly
to ensure my guilt.

December

I was just thinking
it ought to be dark out
by now, which it wasn't,
but then it was. I turn
the lights on, which only
exacerbates the situation.
Some of us are not
doing presents this year.

January

Should have been left blank
but things are still happening.
I attend my sister's cats daily—
they are expectant, grateful as gods.
Geese fly over, having no time
for meaning anything,
being busy organising
against—or is it with?—the seasons.
The river threatens to overstep
but it stays its course,
of course—its course being
wherever it wants to be.

February

New insult: as vibrant
as the North Sea in February.
Like all the best insults
it is local, temporal,
an air balloon
borne entirely
on a precise arrangement
of the atmosphere
and the jettisoning
of unnecessary weight.
Some black-headed gulls
get their black heads back.

March

It is too much
this beginning,
this order.

Just as dawn's first declarations
must come to nothing...
Yet on the thermals
all's vernal,
buzzards and grass
chancing upwards
following a stored feeling.

April

Spring spoke too soon
but bluebells are some announcement
and the months
must happen in their allotted order,
while the seasons do as they please:
a swallow, and another.

May

The ground seems too hard
for anything to grow
but it does, or it does
where the ground allows it.
Mayflies!

June

The marsh quietens.
Solstice slips by in heatwave.
With as little warning,
ducklings appear and disappear.

July

Men from the Environment Agency arrive,
announce special measures.
The river is green at the gills.
Yet there are new arrivals:
a couple of juvenile gadwall,
a female tufted duck.
And the clouds of insects
as thick as the duckweed;
at dusk the fish and bats mark out
the surface of the water from either side.

August

A creche of 77 Canada geese
cross under one bridge
then another, in file formation,
through the stratified duckweed,
carefully avoiding the pumped
spray of water that is no
substitute for rain
or flow.

September

Perhaps things will be better then?
Milder warmth, rain. *Next month,*
we say, *when things calm down…*

Schreckstoff

I was going to write a poem called
'The Summer the Fish Died'.

It would have a sort of sad finality
that was somehow calming. Because,

in geological terms, this is not an event.
It was hot for a long time. Then rain came

down like the upper hand in a slow clap.
But what if the fish die every summer?

What if there are no fish left?
And it is still that summer and every day

more dead fish arrive from upstream.
I want to hold them, and I want

them gone. I cannot smell a living
fish. Perhaps if I was fishier: all tongue,

muscle, tooth and fear. If I had the sense,
could feel the shift of things coming

or missing. If I too were born with
my armour on, it would not save me.

Course

This morning the still river served up
a surplus of shelduck, so many my mind
ran fowl—chewing over their muddled taste.
The gullet has a canniness beyond the brain's.
I was caught with feathers round my gills,
gristle in my evolvéd teeth. For starters,
I forced down that guilty mouthful: gritgrit.
I want to eat what the river gives me. It gives me
assiette of dirts (locally sourced when available).

Gull-billed Tern

Observed on Twitter, an anti-chronological collage

No sign. Has the Gull Billed Tern
been reported there today?
Still here. An early start this morning.
Showed well and heard calling.
Great moment. Reasonable views. Thrilled!
Great bird UK tick, a proper twitch.
Still at Dam end showing well still.
Present, some rather tasty views.
Showing well in moult hence why it's staying still.
Outfall and fishing right over our heads
too close to photograph.
Relieved to have finally caught up with
on railings on pier near dam.
Still dam end showing well!
Still present, flypast at the dam end.
Poor quality shot.
No gull-billed tern visible here!
Great close views... Sweltering heat! Still... still...
On water tower railings. Hot day.
Showing well but in challenging light conditions.
It eventually showed well but was absent for long periods.
More good views, lovely evening light.
For a third night it appears to be roosting
in its usual spot. A rare twitch. Record shots.
Saw it by the skin of my teeth.
Still showing on outfall railings.
Showing nicely favouring the Valve Tower railings.
Still... currently on railing of draw off tower.
Managed a quick video. Was well worth it.

Nice to connect. Tick. By the skin of my teeth.
Wasn't expecting a reappearance.
Fantastically close. The A12 was horrendous.
Another mad rush. Handy little after work twitch.
Still present. OOOOF. A life tick
Gull-billed Tern at Alton Water Dam End.
Now at Dam end perched on valve tower.
No sign. Gull-billed Tern at Alton Water yesterday!

Defences

I read a book:

Der Schimmelreiter by Theodor Storm (1817-88), in English known as *The Dykemaster* though the literal translation is 'Rider on a White Horse'. I found out about the novelle in an essay on 'Dirt Theory'

and in the edition I subsequently sourced there are maps illustrating the former topography of the 'Wattenmeer' (North Sea Flats) and the land, including the Hauke-Haien-Polder with the diverted watercourse. This landscape has been greatly altered

as the translator, writing his preface in the middle of the final decade of the last century, notes, also stating it has been some years since the last English translation appeared and his labour has been a long but rewarding one.

He goes on to explain how the author based his story on a magazine article, 'The Ghostly Rider', an article (now lost) he had read in his great-grandmother's house half a century before. So, the book commences with Storm's narrator recalling reading a piece,

in which the fictionalised writer of the article tells a tale from 'the third decade of the present century' (we might infer further decades had already passed)

in which the protagonist stumbles on a meeting of the dyke committee in a tavern. Sheltering from a storm, he converses with the Dykemaster, who tells him to speak to the old schoolmaster.

'In the middle of the last century...' begins the schoolmaster and, behind the doors, across the marsh, beyond the old and new walls,

we hear the sea.

British Xylonite Co Ltd

It all happened in one go:
the marriage, the job, the move.
The first day, he bought her a comb—

see it looks like tortoiseshell,
but it isn't tortoiseshell.
No need, any longer, to travel,

they can make pretty much
anything: knife handles, cuffs,
film, billiard balls. This stuff

comes from plants. He tried
to explain. Not just a trade,
he was working for change.

He tells her the names—Ivoride,
Celluloid, Lactoid, Xylonite—
but cannot describe

the satisfaction of edges,
the shine inside himself
at the touch, how it *felt*

—total clarity, complete opacity.
It doesn't matter, he is happy
and around the factory

the bright village grows,
solid, lit, lovely houses—
he wants to keep things just so.

Bar Mix

On December days
the sun stops by
just once. Customers
arrive in flurries. Although
they don't always talk,
they tolerate closeness—
like puffed-up garden birds
at feeders. From jars
thick sticky flakes
of corn and rice—
somehow the irregular pieces
settle neatly enough in bowls.

Teneral

How wrong they were,
the old poets.
Round here there are still people
who remember people
who sat with their pints watching
as a boy fell from the sky.

(Actually he jumped,
as the plane—not 40 minutes
from take-off—
failed (all metal is weak).
And this the only survivor,
landed on the bridge's
unexpectant palm
tangled in a parachute
like a mayfly un-emerging.)

The same people
who remember those people
searched themselves
for the wreckage on the marsh,
for the remnants
of that trial disaster.
You can't begrudge them that.
Things are always happening,
people are always there, watching,
thinking 'How extraordinary'.

(And miracles like boys
baled out on bridges
might not take, those boys
might only live long enough
to write to the sister of one of the deceased

(*I trust you will understand me*)
and then fall where there is no bridge,
no onlookers, no one saying
'I've never seen the like'.)

Street Furniture Enthusiast

O verticals, horizontals, dished concrete plantless planters!
The old village pump!
Streetlights!
O VR letterbox!
Signage!
Unbeautiful only surviving instance of this Perspex phone
   box!
O local variation on a theme!
The standard for the years 1970 to '73!
Endless methods for slowing traffic or pedestrians!
O cycle rack!
Mock Tudor public lavatories!
The idealism of drinking fountains!
O to be so charmed by the existence of things
that you always walk down the same street twice!
Reference numbers! Ornate grates! Defunct trademarks!
O safety specifications!
Bollards through the ages!
Bench with dedication!
O to gape like a bin and keep gaping!

Bloody Point:
The First Battle of the River Stour 885

... brocen wurde
'The Battle of Maldon'

What
was broken
What
was fought
What
was where
Who
did boast
Who
did spike
Who
was split
was spilt
What
warriors
What
words
What
war
Which side
were we
What
lost
What
won
Were
we to walk

to look
What
would we find
What
wonder
What
wound
What
Bloody Point

Mehalah: Will

drawn from the novel by Sabine Baring Gould

oh, you have a will
indeed a will
it would be a pleasure to break it will
be a very convenient thing whether you will
be happy I want to see how it will
look in the sun the sun will
be set in a minute I will
go home her stubborn will
will hold to Glory she will
forgive you she will
fall on your neck and ask your pardon the sea will
give up her dead after a storm the sun will
grow sad at heart there will
be a great flare and blaze and glory they will
be in heaven they will
run into one, and that will
be the end there'll
be an end of this world with fierce will
if I draw in with my will
my will can burst them open my will
can wrench them off against my will
but come of your own free will
my will is gaining your will
is stout you'll
come together all the faster for it will
marry you will
not marry him will
never marry you I'll
tell you what he will

carry out will
draw the teeth out of your gums we will
go together to her it will
not fall apart it will

Ad Ansam

Literally—
'before the opportunity'—
or 'before
the Stour'—before the Stour
was 'the Stour'—
or by—or next—or on—or
'at the bend'—
'at the loop'—
or 'at the handle'—
where the rivers meet—
or roads meet—
a fortress offering—
or requiring—defence—
or 'hanner sau'—
the station half-way—
between London
and Venta Icenorum—
mill pond—
mill race—
a weir—
where I have walked—
have swum—
have met—
a suggested end—
or starting point—
along *the Sture*—
that parteth with
his pleasant Floods—
though here the Stour
is narrow—ford-able—
is Stratford—the crossing
at the street—or river—

or is Higham—a hedged
or enclosed dwelling—
is ingress and egress—
portage place—a parking spot—
St Mary, deliver us—safely
off the A12—St Mary, protect us—
from Himalayan balsam—
from spate and indifference—
provide a chance—
for mayflies—
and their predators—
a stop—along the way—

The Great Consternation

22 April, 1884: Mr George Stebbing arranges a pyramid of tinned lobster in his window, as carefully as the dressings of state. Everything pink and clean in the sun; his head, the lobster meat, his scrubbed hands. From here he can see Lord Alfred Paget aboard his fine yacht. He cannot see back the other way about the globe, but he knows it is a British world. He hums.

You could tell it was precisely 9.18am GMT, as that was when the Great Consternation struck. It was felt throughout the counties but its centre was at Colchester, and here in Wivenhoe.

Mr Stebbing felt compelled, like many of his contemporaries, to lie down with some speed and force. Here he could observe the tins bounce and roll about the floor of his shop. At that moment, though he could not have known, thousands across Essex and Suffolk found they too no longer wished to stand. For three minutes the earth moved out of time with the towers of churches and window displays, and men lay on their bellies. The cracks can still be seen today.

East Atlantic Flyway

I forgot to note the date
those honking great skeins
of geese came in, spooling and unspooling
their arrival—milking it, you might say.
Blown in like a blewse,
settling on the scald of the hill
like spatfall. Noisy buggers.
And I forgot to count,
to take account, to calculate
if more had become fewer or vice versa
as they ravelled up the estuary,
regardless of the shoaly bits
the boat-bound must avoid
at all costs, so deadly they named them:
The Altar, The Glutton, The Gristle, The Bore.
A simpler life: to re-mulch the mud,
to graze the grasses which best
suit, to stop of your own pleasing:
this podzol, that stubble,
without ever asking 'Who owns
this field? Whose gleanings
are these?' To travel so far
and no fudder. To travel
in kiddles, whiffling wanderers,
struck out like fish traps,
fish ladders, a complex system
of watermills becoming problematic
to migrating fish from as early
as the 11th century. They pay no
rent or expenses, no fish silver.
Nawthing. Not done a day's work
in all their life. Take, take, take,

and take off. Furreners.
I've seen them myself; nullius
in verba, buddy. Oh no,
muchos muchos in verba, buh,
this muddy data stream
flooding our demesne.

Black Tern

A washout. Through the rain,
through the bins, each tern was black
then grey, then black, then probably
a Common, or an Arctic. Yes, definitely.
The rain found its way into our macs
until it no longer mattered, we were soaked,
totally, and the terns—darkly wheeling—
were also a sight. And even perched,
familiar on the outflow tower, worth
a look. Jeans drying stiff by the pub fire
my toes curled and squelched as I began
to believe all the birds were out there
and we'd see them eventually—the regulars,
the rarities. This climate could be perfect,
we wouldn't lose a single species
but still the new ones would come:
White-tailed eagle, Great auk, every tern.

A Boundary Dispute

A bit further out, up
where Suffolk and Norfolk
meet, a blind man
once slept, or slipped,
between two parishes,
at the Dolphin Inn,
where each year the bounds
were beat, along
the line of a ceiling beam.

Across that line,
one Thomas Woods, pauper,
took his rest, but could
not settle, his head
and body being separate.
Where does this person
belong? Can there be
relief? The Courts'
decision does not appear.

We must draw the line somewhere.
So let us make a rolling fence,
whereby the cuttings
from your hedge
are thrown beyond,
and so, by increments,
our edges move—

or let us click, unzoom,
and see it's not so far,
really, we could go—
except The Manor House,
(renamed) is permanently

closed. So that's that, unless
you can suggest an edit.

It's Not Over Yet

Thing is, in April or May, when the Hoary cress appears, I'm already picturing her younger, leggier cousin: Dittander, froth of full summer. If the older is crucifer, bearing the cross, Dittander is the brass in brassica, the fin-de-siècle attitude; petticoats to the sky in cancan. So here I am in springtime, wishing for the brink of autumn, because I see it coming—the serrated spears piercing the seawall.

Goosefoot

i.m. TH

It's the prospect

The paths opening before you

Three types of goosefoot

    The patte d'oie of stately stops on long drives
    The Stinking goosefoot of nose-wrinkling rarity
    The actual goose with its actual foot

\|/

    We'll wander back to that summer we spent
    Searching for the mealy annual
    Prostrate to erect

      Smelling strongly of rotting fish
      I had found a new enthusiasm
      And made you follow it

        Every week round the rifle butts
        Ranging the kicked shingle
        Scuffed sandy earth

          Between the tangled mounds
          I have not found another way than this
          To find it you must first picture it

            Then every glance is an empty frame

            Every space choked with disappointment

            A thousand tiny griefs burring every scene

***

Just as we're heading home
I see and know it at once
Already an old friend

> Much reduced now
> But entirely itself
> Nothing quite like it

How could I not have seen it before?

And there too, and there

Where the rubbed path splits

\|/

We're younger
Making the most of our family membership
Stopping here on the way to the holiday proper

And I am impatient for seaside
But delighted with parquetry
Trail in hand

Serious intent

Off to find the folly

And then the patte d'oie

My acheless legs enjoying
The agony of options
Retracing my steps

Running back to the beginning

Wanting to get moving

And not wanting to leave one path unknown

So much started there
The vanishing point of my obsessions
Paths which opened for me

\|/

Now here I am
The slapping reality of a goose's foot
Slamming the mud of summer

This time of year
Just the familiar foreigns become permanent residents
Canada, Egyptian

The occasional greylag, the lagging brent
Tide out they lay a track in warm silt
A muddle of paths

Each made up of a thousand trifurcated footprints
And this repeated in every estuary
The scheme submerged and re-begun twice a day

The daily slog and sludge of this

Even this I would want to share with you

Which brings me back to the central point

The paths
The paths that branch from them
You have to picture it

Spaces

Ways to go forward

And back. And back again

Notes

'At Cobbold Point' takes its riff from Tom Williamson's *Sandlands: The Suffolk Coast and Heaths* (Windgather Press, 2005).

'The Age of Coastal Sail' draws on many books about East Anglia, but special mention must be given to the incredible work of Hervey Benham (1910–1987).

'Don the Diver' is a true story... perhaps. The facts, such as they are, came to me through a piece in the *Ipswich Journal*, 15 July 1848.

'Survivors of the East Coast Floods': I am especially indebted to Dorothy Summers' book *The East Coast Floods* (David & Charles, 1978) for information on the tragic events of 1953.

'Superstant' takes the particulars of an old custom and the idea of such customs in general from the work of George Ewart Evans (1909–1988).

'Suffolk Girls' collages descriptions, including those of horses and women, in *The History of Margaret Catchpole*.

'Smugglers' includes items purloined from a great many books, notably John Leather's *The Northseamen* (Terence Dalton Ltd, 1971).

'Starfish' began with an attempted walk to the Second World War QF and QL bombing decoy located at East Mersea (TM 052 157). These 'starfish' sites used fires and mirrors to disorientate enemy bombers and deflect attacks on important ports.

'Schreckstoff', from the German meaning 'scary stuff', is a chemical alarm signal, a pheromone released by the specialised skin cells of certain fish when they are damaged.

'Defences' mainly cites its sources, but the essay referred to is 'Dirt Theory and Material Ecocriticism' by Hannah I. Sullivan (2012).

'Teneral' takes as its basis a tale I think I originally heard at my local. At the least, stories of wreckage on Cattawade Marshes from a RAF plane crash in 1942 led me to various discussions on internet forums and from there to an entry on ipswichwarmemorial.co.uk, which lists the deceased as: Wilfred John Ferris 'Tink', Bertram Scott Watt Grieve, Frederick Rex Higgott, Alan Mahoney, Leslie Nockels, Walter McNaught Thompson and Norman Holland Simms. The surviving serviceman, George Allan Hinshelwood, was killed a year later in the Netherlands.

'Mehalah: Will' collages phrases from the novel that contain the word 'will'.

'Ad Ansam' paddles about in the murky geography and etymology of a Roman fort that once stood somewhere around the Suffolk villages of Stratford St Mary and Higham.

The quote comes from Edmund Spenser's *Faerie Queene*, Book IV: The Sture, that parteth with his pleasant Floods / The eastern Saxons from the southern ny, / And Clare and Harwitch both doth beautify'.

'The Great Consternation' takes as its title a phrase used repeatedly in an anonymous contemporary report in the *Essex Chronicle* of Friday 25 April 1884, reproduced in *Earthquake in Essex 1884: A unique record of an historic occurrence* (Westcliff Litho Company, 1974).

'A Boundary Dispute' was born of general reading and settled in an account in *The Betts of Wortham in Suffolk, 1480–1905* by Katharine Frances Doughty (The Bodley Head, 1912).

Acknowledgements

Enormous thanks are due to Cove Park and The Fenton Arts Trust for an Early Career Residency in September 2018, where this collection was first conceived and without which it likely would not exist.

Thanks to the following publications where some of these poems, or previous versions of them, have appeared: *Finished Creatures, Poetry Birmingham Literary Journal, Poetry London, Prototype 4, The Tangerine.*

Thank you to Deryn, Alison, Lydia and Melissa and all the Pavilion team for their support, patience and belief.

Thank you to Polly Atkin, Isabel Galleymore, Jenny 'Jen' Holden, Declan Ryan, and Kathryn Maris for generously giving their time and valuable insight to these poems.

I read a great deal when writing and thinking about this book. Some of that reading has washed up here in a recognisable form as evidenced in the Notes, but much else had a broader, less quantifiable influence. Immeasurable thanks is owed to those 'local' authors whose research informs me and enthusiasm moves me; the small presses and printers that made the work available; the Suffolk and Essex Library Services, particularly the staff at Manningtree Library, for access to these treasures; and to the loved ones of the authors who must surely have put up with a great deal—which reminds me...

Thanks, most of all, to the friends and family who have been there for me, especially my mum, sister, brother-in-law and nibling. I am grateful always to my beloved and brilliant late father who must take a large portion of the blame for me turning out to be a poet. And to my partner, Claire: thank you, for everything.